50 Premium Japanese Sandwich Recipes

By: Kelly Johnson

Table of Contents

- Katsu Sando (Pork Cutlet Sandwich)
- Tamago Sando (Japanese Egg Sandwich)
- Ebi Katsu Sando (Shrimp Cutlet Sandwich)
- Teriyaki Chicken Sando
- Tuna Salad Sando with Wasabi
- Shabu-Shabu Sando
- Miso-Marinated Salmon Sando
- Beef Sukiyaki Sando
- Yakitori Chicken Sando
- Sweet Potato and Avocado Sando
- Karaage Chicken Sando
- Spicy Tofu and Cucumber Sando
- Shiso and Umeboshi Sando
- Crab Salad Sando
- Unagi (Grilled Eel) Sando
- Japanese Curry Chicken Sando
- Grilled Vegetable Sando
- Pork and Kimchi Sando
- Roasted Beef and Wasabi Sando
- Soft Shell Crab Sando
- Grilled Cheese with Miso Sando
- Spam and Fried Egg Sando
- Chashu Pork Sando
- Shrimp Tempura Sando
- Curry Udon Sando
- Salmon Roe and Cream Cheese Sando
- Ramen Burger Sando
- Japanese Caesar Salad Sando
- Yakiniku Beef Sando
- Avocado and Teriyaki Chicken Sando
- Tofu Katsu Sando
- Prawn and Avocado Sando
- Sweet Bean Paste (Anko) Sando
- Okonomiyaki Sando
- Wasabi Tuna Tartare Sando

- Japanese Cheeseburger Sando
- Grilled Salmon and Pickled Ginger Sando
- Tsukune (Chicken Meatball) Sando
- Pickled Plum and Pork Sando
- Roasted Duck and Plum Sauce Sando
- Spicy Miso and Eggplant Sando
- Agedashi Tofu Sando
- Spicy Shrimp and Cabbage Sando
- Tofu and Avocado Miso Sando
- Mentaiko (Cod Roe) Sando
- Grilled Chicken and Pickled Radish Sando
- Japanese Hot Dog Sando
- Udon and Tempura Sando
- Katsuobushi (Dried Bonito Flakes) and Avocado Sando
- Gyu Don (Beef Rice Bowl) Sando

Katsu Sando (Pork Cutlet Sandwich)

Ingredients:

- 2 slices of soft white bread
- 1 pork cutlet (tonkatsu, breaded and fried)
- 1 tablespoon tonkatsu sauce
- 1 tablespoon mayonnaise
- Shredded cabbage

Instructions:

1. Fry the pork cutlet until golden and crispy.
2. Mix the tonkatsu sauce and mayonnaise together.
3. Toast the bread lightly.
4. Spread the sauce-mayo mixture on both slices of bread.
5. Place the pork cutlet on the bread and top with shredded cabbage.
6. Close the sandwich and serve.

Tamago Sando (Japanese Egg Sandwich)

Ingredients:

- 2 slices of soft white bread
- 2 eggs
- 1 tablespoon mayonnaise
- 1 teaspoon Dijon mustard (optional)
- Salt and pepper to taste

Instructions:

1. Beat the eggs with a pinch of salt and pepper.
2. Cook the eggs in a non-stick pan, stirring constantly to create soft scrambled eggs.
3. Once cooked, mix in the mayonnaise and Dijon mustard.
4. Spread the egg mixture on one slice of bread and top with the other slice.
5. Cut into halves or quarters to serve.

Ebi Katsu Sando (Shrimp Cutlet Sandwich)

Ingredients:

- 2 slices of soft white bread
- 6 large shrimp, breaded and fried (ebi katsu)
- 1 tablespoon tartar sauce
- Shredded lettuce

Instructions:

1. Bread and fry the shrimp until golden.
2. Spread tartar sauce on both slices of bread.
3. Place the fried shrimp on one slice of bread and top with shredded lettuce.
4. Close the sandwich and serve.

Teriyaki Chicken Sando

Ingredients:

- 2 slices of soft white bread
- 1 grilled chicken breast, sliced
- 2 tablespoons teriyaki sauce
- Shredded lettuce
- Sliced cucumber

Instructions:

1. Grill the chicken and brush it with teriyaki sauce during the final minute of cooking.
2. Toast the bread slices lightly.
3. Spread some extra teriyaki sauce on the bread.
4. Layer the chicken slices, shredded lettuce, and cucumber on the bread.
5. Close the sandwich and serve.

Tuna Salad Sando with Wasabi

Ingredients:

- 2 slices of soft white bread
- 1 can of tuna, drained
- 1 tablespoon mayonnaise
- 1 teaspoon wasabi paste
- 1/4 cup chopped celery
- Salt and pepper to taste

Instructions:

1. Mix the tuna with mayonnaise, wasabi paste, chopped celery, salt, and pepper.
2. Spread the tuna salad on one slice of bread.
3. Top with the second slice of bread and serve.

Shabu-Shabu Sando

Ingredients:

- 2 slices of soft white bread
- Thinly sliced beef (shabu-shabu style)
- 1 tablespoon ponzu sauce
- Shredded cabbage
- 1 teaspoon sesame oil

Instructions:

1. Lightly cook the beef slices in hot water for shabu-shabu.
2. Toss the beef in ponzu sauce and sesame oil.
3. Toast the bread lightly.
4. Layer the beef and shredded cabbage on one slice of bread.
5. Close the sandwich and serve.

Miso-Marinated Salmon Sando

Ingredients:

- 2 slices of soft white bread
- 1 piece of salmon fillet
- 2 tablespoons miso paste
- 1 teaspoon sesame oil
- Sliced cucumber
- Shredded lettuce

Instructions:

1. Marinate the salmon in miso paste and sesame oil for 30 minutes.
2. Grill or pan-sear the salmon until cooked through.
3. Toast the bread lightly.
4. Place the salmon on the bread, top with cucumber and lettuce.
5. Close the sandwich and serve.

Beef Sukiyaki Sando

Ingredients:

- 2 slices of soft white bread
- 100g thinly sliced beef (sukiyaki style)
- 2 tablespoons soy sauce
- 1 tablespoon mirin
- 1 tablespoon sugar
- Shredded green onions

Instructions:

1. Cook the beef in a pan with soy sauce, mirin, and sugar until tender.
2. Toast the bread slices lightly.
3. Place the cooked beef on one slice of bread, and garnish with shredded green onions.
4. Close the sandwich and serve.

Yakitori Chicken Sando

Ingredients:

- 2 slices of soft white bread
- 1 grilled chicken skewer (yakitori), sliced
- 1 tablespoon tare sauce (yakitori sauce)
- Sliced scallions

Instructions:

1. Grill the chicken on skewers and baste with tare sauce.
2. Toast the bread lightly.
3. Slice the grilled chicken and place on one slice of bread.
4. Drizzle with more tare sauce and top with sliced scallions.
5. Close the sandwich and serve.

Sweet Potato and Avocado Sando

Ingredients:

- 2 slices of soft white bread
- 1 small sweet potato, roasted and mashed
- 1 ripe avocado, sliced
- 1 tablespoon tahini or olive oil
- Salt and pepper to taste
- A squeeze of lemon juice

Instructions:

1. Roast the sweet potato until soft, then mash with a little tahini or olive oil.
2. Toast the bread lightly.
3. Spread the mashed sweet potato on one slice of bread.
4. Layer with sliced avocado, seasoning with salt, pepper, and a squeeze of lemon juice.
5. Close the sandwich and serve.

Karaage Chicken Sando

Ingredients:

- 2 slices of soft white bread
- 1 piece of karaage chicken (Japanese fried chicken)
- 1 tablespoon mayonnaise
- Shredded lettuce
- 1 tablespoon tonkatsu sauce (optional)

Instructions:

1. Prepare or buy karaage chicken and fry it until crispy.
2. Toast the bread lightly.
3. Spread mayonnaise on both slices of bread.
4. Place the karaage chicken on the bread, top with shredded lettuce, and drizzle with tonkatsu sauce (optional).
5. Close the sandwich and serve.

Spicy Tofu and Cucumber Sando

Ingredients:

- 2 slices of soft white bread
- 1/2 block of firm tofu, pressed and sliced
- 1 tablespoon soy sauce
- 1 teaspoon chili paste (or sriracha)
- 1/2 cucumber, thinly sliced
- A handful of fresh cilantro

Instructions:

1. Press and slice the tofu, then cook it in a hot pan with soy sauce and chili paste until crispy on both sides.
2. Toast the bread lightly.
3. Spread a small amount of soy sauce or additional chili paste on the bread.
4. Layer the tofu and cucumber slices on one slice of bread, and garnish with fresh cilantro.
5. Close the sandwich and serve.

Shiso and Umeboshi Sando

Ingredients:

- 2 slices of soft white bread
- 5-6 fresh shiso leaves
- 1-2 umeboshi plums (pickled plums), mashed
- 1 tablespoon mayonnaise

Instructions:

1. Toast the bread lightly.
2. Spread mashed umeboshi plum on one slice of bread.
3. Layer with fresh shiso leaves and drizzle a little mayonnaise.
4. Close the sandwich and serve.

Crab Salad Sando

Ingredients:

- 2 slices of soft white bread
- 100g cooked crab meat (or imitation crab)
- 2 tablespoons mayonnaise
- 1 teaspoon Dijon mustard (optional)
- 1 tablespoon chopped celery
- A pinch of lemon juice

Instructions:

1. Mix the crab meat with mayonnaise, Dijon mustard (optional), chopped celery, and a squeeze of lemon juice.
2. Toast the bread lightly.
3. Spread the crab salad on one slice of bread.
4. Top with the second slice of bread and serve.

Unagi (Grilled Eel) Sando

Ingredients:

- 2 slices of soft white bread
- 1 piece of grilled unagi (eel)
- 2 tablespoons eel sauce (unagi no tare)
- 1 tablespoon toasted sesame seeds

Instructions:

1. Grill or pan-sear the unagi and baste with eel sauce.
2. Toast the bread lightly.
3. Place the grilled eel on the bread and drizzle with extra eel sauce.
4. Sprinkle with toasted sesame seeds.
5. Close the sandwich and serve.

Japanese Curry Chicken Sando

Ingredients:

- 2 slices of soft white bread
- 1 chicken breast, cooked and sliced
- 1/4 cup Japanese curry sauce (use leftover curry or pre-made curry paste)
- Shredded cabbage

Instructions:

1. Heat the chicken and curry sauce together in a pan.
2. Toast the bread lightly.
3. Spread a little curry sauce on the bread.
4. Place the sliced chicken and top with shredded cabbage.
5. Close the sandwich and serve.

Grilled Vegetable Sando

Ingredients:

- 2 slices of soft white bread
- 1 small zucchini, sliced
- 1 small eggplant, sliced
- 1 red bell pepper, sliced
- 1 tablespoon olive oil
- 1 tablespoon balsamic vinegar
- Salt and pepper to taste

Instructions:

1. Toss the vegetables in olive oil, balsamic vinegar, salt, and pepper.
2. Grill the vegetables until tender and slightly charred.
3. Toast the bread lightly.
4. Layer the grilled vegetables on one slice of bread.
5. Close the sandwich and serve.

Pork and Kimchi Sando

Ingredients:

- 2 slices of soft white bread
- 1 pork cutlet, cooked
- 1/4 cup kimchi, chopped
- 1 tablespoon mayonnaise
- 1 teaspoon sriracha (optional)

Instructions:

1. Cook the pork cutlet and toast the bread lightly.
2. Mix mayonnaise with sriracha (if using).
3. Spread the mayo mixture on the bread.
4. Layer the pork cutlet with chopped kimchi on one slice of bread.
5. Close the sandwich and serve.

Roasted Beef and Wasabi Sando

Ingredients:

- 2 slices of soft white bread
- 100g roasted beef, thinly sliced
- 1 tablespoon wasabi mayonnaise (mix wasabi with mayo)
- Fresh arugula or spinach leaves

Instructions:

1. Toast the bread lightly.
2. Spread wasabi mayonnaise on both slices of bread.
3. Layer the roasted beef slices and add fresh greens.
4. Close the sandwich and serve.

Soft Shell Crab Sando

Ingredients:

- 2 slices of soft white bread
- 2 soft-shell crabs, deep-fried
- 1 tablespoon tartar sauce
- Shredded lettuce
- Slices of cucumber

Instructions:

1. Deep-fry the soft-shell crabs until crispy.
2. Toast the bread lightly.
3. Spread tartar sauce on the bread.
4. Layer the crispy crabs, shredded lettuce, and cucumber slices.
5. Close the sandwich and serve.

Grilled Cheese with Miso Sando

Ingredients:

- 2 slices of thick white or sourdough bread
- 2 slices of cheddar cheese
- 1 tablespoon white miso paste
- 1 tablespoon butter

Instructions:

1. Spread a thin layer of miso paste on one side of the bread slices.
2. Place the cheddar cheese between the slices of bread.
3. Butter the outside of the bread.
4. Grill the sandwich in a pan until golden brown and the cheese is melted.
5. Serve hot.

Spam and Fried Egg Sando

Ingredients:

- 2 slices of soft white bread
- 2 slices of Spam, fried
- 1 fried egg
- 1 tablespoon mayonnaise or Kewpie mayo

Instructions:

1. Fry the Spam slices until crispy.
2. Fry an egg to your desired doneness.
3. Toast the bread lightly.
4. Spread mayonnaise on both slices of bread.
5. Layer the fried Spam and egg in the sandwich.
6. Close and serve.

Chashu Pork Sando

Ingredients:

- 2 slices of soft white bread
- 2-3 slices of chashu pork (braised pork belly)
- 1 tablespoon soy sauce
- 1 tablespoon hoisin sauce
- Shredded cabbage

Instructions:

1. Braise or pan-sear the chashu pork until tender.
2. Toast the bread lightly.
3. Drizzle soy sauce and hoisin sauce on one slice of bread.
4. Layer the chashu pork and top with shredded cabbage.
5. Close the sandwich and serve.

Shrimp Tempura Sando

Ingredients:

- 2 slices of soft white bread
- 3-4 pieces of shrimp tempura
- 1 tablespoon tartar sauce or eel sauce
- Shredded lettuce

Instructions:

1. Fry the shrimp tempura until crispy.
2. Toast the bread lightly.
3. Spread tartar sauce or eel sauce on the bread.
4. Layer the shrimp tempura and top with shredded lettuce.
5. Close the sandwich and serve.

Curry Udon Sando

Ingredients:

- 2 slices of soft white bread
- 1/2 cup curry udon (leftover curry udon or prepared curry sauce and udon noodles)
- 1 tablespoon mayonnaise

Instructions:

1. Prepare or reheat curry udon.
2. Toast the bread lightly.
3. Spread mayonnaise on one slice of bread.
4. Layer the curry udon on the bread.
5. Close the sandwich and serve immediately.

Salmon Roe and Cream Cheese Sando

Ingredients:

- 2 slices of soft white bread
- 2 tablespoons cream cheese
- 1 tablespoon salmon roe (ikura)
- Fresh dill or chives

Instructions:

1. Spread cream cheese on both slices of bread.
2. Add a generous spoonful of salmon roe.
3. Garnish with fresh dill or chives.
4. Close the sandwich and serve.

Ramen Burger Sando

Ingredients:

- 2 ramen buns (cook ramen noodles, shape into buns, and pan-fry them)
- 1 beef patty
- 1 tablespoon soy sauce
- 1 tablespoon mayonnaise
- 1/2 cup lettuce, shredded
- 1 slice of tomato

Instructions:

1. Cook ramen noodles and press them into round molds. Pan-fry the ramen buns until crispy.
2. Grill the beef patty and drizzle soy sauce on top.
3. Spread mayonnaise on the ramen buns.
4. Layer the beef patty, shredded lettuce, and tomato slices.
5. Close the ramen buns and serve.

Japanese Caesar Salad Sando

Ingredients:

- 2 slices of soft white bread
- 1 cup romaine lettuce, chopped
- 2 tablespoons Caesar dressing
- 1 tablespoon soy sauce
- 1 tablespoon grated Parmesan cheese

Instructions:

1. Toss the chopped lettuce with Caesar dressing, soy sauce, and grated Parmesan cheese.
2. Toast the bread lightly.
3. Pile the dressed salad onto one slice of bread.
4. Close the sandwich and serve.

Yakiniku Beef Sando

Ingredients:

- 2 slices of soft white bread
- 150g yakiniku beef (grilled thinly sliced beef)
- 1 tablespoon yakiniku sauce (soy sauce, sesame oil, garlic, and sugar mix)
- Shredded cabbage
- 1 tablespoon mayonnaise

Instructions:

1. Grill the beef and brush it with yakiniku sauce during cooking.
2. Toast the bread lightly.
3. Spread mayonnaise on one slice of bread.
4. Layer the yakiniku beef and top with shredded cabbage.
5. Close the sandwich and serve.

Avocado and Teriyaki Chicken Sando

Ingredients:

- 2 slices of soft white bread
- 1 grilled chicken breast
- 1/2 avocado, sliced
- 2 tablespoons teriyaki sauce
- Shredded lettuce

Instructions:

1. Grill the chicken breast and drizzle with teriyaki sauce.
2. Toast the bread lightly.
3. Layer the teriyaki chicken, avocado slices, and shredded lettuce.
4. Close the sandwich and serve.

Tofu Katsu Sando

Ingredients:

- 2 slices of soft white bread
- 1 block of firm tofu, sliced
- 1/4 cup panko breadcrumbs
- 1 egg (for batter)
- 1 tablespoon tonkatsu sauce
- Shredded cabbage

Instructions:

1. Dip the tofu slices into beaten egg and coat with panko breadcrumbs.
2. Fry the tofu slices until crispy and golden brown.
3. Toast the bread lightly.
4. Spread tonkatsu sauce on one slice of bread.
5. Layer the crispy tofu and top with shredded cabbage.
6. Close the sandwich and serve.

Prawn and Avocado Sando

Ingredients:

- 2 slices of soft white bread
- 6-8 cooked prawns
- 1/2 avocado, sliced
- 1 tablespoon mayonnaise
- Fresh coriander

Instructions:

1. Toast the bread lightly.
2. Spread mayonnaise on both slices of bread.
3. Layer the prawns and avocado slices.
4. Garnish with fresh coriander.
5. Close the sandwich and serve.

Sweet Bean Paste (Anko) Sando

Ingredients:

- 2 slices of soft white bread
- 2-3 tablespoons sweet red bean paste (anko)
- 1 tablespoon butter (optional)

Instructions:

1. Toast the bread lightly (optional: spread a thin layer of butter on the bread before toasting).
2. Spread the sweet red bean paste on one slice of bread.
3. Close the sandwich and serve.

Okonomiyaki Sando

Ingredients:

- 2 slices of soft white bread
- 1 small okonomiyaki pancake (Japanese savory pancake)
- Okonomiyaki sauce (or Worcestershire sauce)
- Bonito flakes and aonori (dried seaweed)

Instructions:

1. Make okonomiyaki pancakes with your choice of ingredients (cabbage, pork, or seafood).
2. Toast the bread lightly.
3. Place the okonomiyaki pancake on one slice of bread and drizzle with okonomiyaki sauce.
4. Sprinkle bonito flakes and aonori on top.
5. Close the sandwich and serve.

Wasabi Tuna Tartare Sando

Ingredients:

- 2 slices of soft white bread
- 100g raw tuna, finely chopped
- 1 teaspoon wasabi paste
- 1 tablespoon soy sauce
- 1 tablespoon sesame oil
- Cucumber slices

Instructions:

1. Mix the chopped tuna with wasabi paste, soy sauce, and sesame oil.
2. Toast the bread lightly.
3. Spread the tuna tartare on one slice of bread and top with cucumber slices.
4. Close the sandwich and serve.

Japanese Cheeseburger Sando

Ingredients:

- 2 slices of soft white bread or burger bun
- 1 beef patty (seasoned with soy sauce and mirin)
- 1 slice of cheddar or Japanese melting cheese (like mozzarella)
- 1 tablespoon tonkatsu sauce
- Pickled cucumbers or Japanese pickles (takuan)

Instructions:

1. Grill the beef patty and melt the cheese on top.
2. Toast the bread or bun lightly.
3. Spread tonkatsu sauce on the bread.
4. Layer the beef patty, melted cheese, and pickled cucumbers.
5. Close the sandwich and serve.

Grilled Salmon and Pickled Ginger Sando

Ingredients:

- 2 slices of soft white bread
- 1 grilled salmon fillet
- 1 tablespoon pickled ginger, sliced
- 1 tablespoon mayonnaise
- Fresh spinach or arugula

Instructions:

1. Grill the salmon fillet and break it into pieces.
2. Toast the bread lightly.
3. Spread mayonnaise on both slices of bread.
4. Layer the grilled salmon, pickled ginger, and fresh spinach or arugula.
5. Close the sandwich and serve.

Tsukune (Chicken Meatball) Sando

Ingredients:

- 2 slices of soft white bread
- 3-4 tsukune (chicken meatballs)
- 1 tablespoon tare sauce (soy sauce, mirin, sugar)
- Shredded lettuce
- 1 tablespoon mayonnaise

Instructions:

1. Grill or pan-fry the tsukune until cooked through.
2. Drizzle the tare sauce over the meatballs.
3. Toast the bread lightly.
4. Spread mayonnaise on one slice of bread.
5. Layer the tsukune meatballs and top with shredded lettuce.
6. Close the sandwich and serve.

Pickled Plum and Pork Sando

Ingredients:

- 2 slices of soft white bread
- 150g grilled pork tenderloin or tonkatsu
- 1 tablespoon pickled umeboshi (plum paste)
- Shredded cabbage

Instructions:

1. Grill or pan-fry the pork until tender.
2. Toast the bread lightly.
3. Spread umeboshi paste on one slice of bread.
4. Layer the grilled pork and top with shredded cabbage.
5. Close the sandwich and serve.

Roasted Duck and Plum Sauce Sando

Ingredients:

- 2 slices of soft white bread
- 1/2 roasted duck breast, sliced
- 2 tablespoons plum sauce
- Fresh cilantro or parsley
- Cucumber slices

Instructions:

1. Roast the duck breast and slice thinly.
2. Toast the bread lightly.
3. Spread plum sauce on one slice of bread.
4. Layer the sliced duck and top with cucumber slices and fresh cilantro or parsley.
5. Close the sandwich and serve.

Spicy Miso and Eggplant Sando

Ingredients:

- 2 slices of soft white bread
- 1 eggplant, sliced into rounds
- 2 tablespoons spicy miso paste
- 1 tablespoon sesame oil
- Fresh cilantro or shiso leaves

Instructions:

1. Grill or pan-fry the eggplant slices with sesame oil until tender.
2. Toast the bread lightly.
3. Spread the spicy miso paste on one slice of bread.
4. Layer the grilled eggplant and top with fresh cilantro or shiso leaves.
5. Close the sandwich and serve.

Agedashi Tofu Sando

Ingredients:

- 2 slices of soft white bread
- 1 block of firm tofu, cut into thick slices
- 1/4 cup potato starch (for frying)
- 2 tablespoons soy sauce
- 1 tablespoon mirin
- 1 tablespoon dashi broth
- Green onions (for garnish)

Instructions:

1. Coat the tofu slices in potato starch and fry until golden brown.
2. In a small saucepan, combine soy sauce, mirin, and dashi to make the sauce.
3. Toast the bread lightly.
4. Place the fried tofu on one slice of bread.
5. Drizzle the soy-mirin-dashi sauce over the tofu and garnish with green onions.
6. Close the sandwich and serve.

Spicy Shrimp and Cabbage Sando

Ingredients:

- 2 slices of soft white bread
- 6-8 cooked shrimp, peeled and deveined
- 1 tablespoon sriracha or chili paste
- 1 tablespoon mayonnaise
- Shredded cabbage
- 1 tablespoon sesame seeds

Instructions:

1. Toss the cooked shrimp in a mix of sriracha or chili paste and mayonnaise.
2. Toast the bread lightly.
3. Spread the spicy shrimp mixture on one slice of bread.
4. Top with shredded cabbage and sesame seeds.
5. Close the sandwich and serve.

Tofu and Avocado Miso Sando

Ingredients:

- 2 slices of soft white bread
- 1/2 avocado, sliced
- 1/2 block firm tofu, sliced
- 1 tablespoon white miso paste
- 1 teaspoon sesame oil
- Fresh spinach or lettuce

Instructions:

1. Pan-fry the tofu slices with sesame oil until golden.
2. Toast the bread lightly.
3. Spread miso paste on one slice of bread.
4. Layer the tofu, avocado slices, and spinach or lettuce.
5. Close the sandwich and serve.

Mentaiko (Cod Roe) Sando

Ingredients:

- 2 slices of soft white bread
- 2 tablespoons mentaiko (cod roe)
- 1 tablespoon mayonnaise
- 1 teaspoon butter (optional)
- Fresh parsley (for garnish)

Instructions:

1. Mix the mentaiko with mayonnaise in a bowl.
2. Toast the bread lightly and spread butter on one slice if desired.
3. Spread the mentaiko-mayo mixture on one slice of bread.
4. Close the sandwich and garnish with fresh parsley if desired.
5. Serve immediately.

Grilled Chicken and Pickled Radish Sando

Ingredients:

- 2 slices of soft white bread
- 1 grilled chicken breast, sliced thin
- 2 tablespoons pickled daikon radish (or regular radish)
- Lettuce leaves
- Japanese mayonnaise (optional)

Instructions:

1. Grill the chicken breast and slice thinly.
2. Toast the bread lightly.
3. Spread mayonnaise on one slice of bread (optional).
4. Layer the sliced grilled chicken and top with pickled radish and lettuce.
5. Close the sandwich and serve.

Japanese Hot Dog Sando

Ingredients:

- 2 slices of soft milk bread
- 1 Japanese-style hot dog (sausages)
- 1 tablespoon tonkatsu sauce
- Shredded cabbage
- Japanese mayonnaise

Instructions:

1. Grill or pan-fry the hot dog sausages.
2. Toast the milk bread lightly.
3. Spread a layer of tonkatsu sauce on one slice of bread.
4. Place the hot dog sausage on the bread and top with shredded cabbage and a drizzle of Japanese mayonnaise.
5. Close the sandwich and serve.

Udon and Tempura Sando

Ingredients:

- 2 slices of soft white bread
- 1 serving of udon noodles (cooked)
- 2-3 pieces of tempura shrimp or vegetables
- Soy sauce or dipping sauce for udon
- Shredded lettuce

Instructions:

1. Cook the udon noodles and tempura shrimp/vegetables.
2. Toast the bread lightly.
3. Place the udon noodles on one slice of bread and drizzle with a bit of soy sauce or dipping sauce.
4. Top with tempura shrimp and shredded lettuce.
5. Close the sandwich and serve immediately.

Katsuobushi (Dried Bonito Flakes) and Avocado Sando

Ingredients:

- 2 slices of soft white bread
- 1/2 avocado, sliced
- 2 tablespoons katsuobushi (dried bonito flakes)
- Soy sauce or ponzu sauce (optional)
- Shiso leaves or lettuce

Instructions:

1. Toast the bread lightly.
2. Spread a thin layer of soy sauce or ponzu sauce on one slice of bread.
3. Layer the sliced avocado and sprinkle katsuobushi over the top.
4. Add fresh shiso leaves or lettuce for extra crunch.
5. Close the sandwich and serve.

Gyu Don (Beef Rice Bowl) Sando

Ingredients:

- 2 slices of soft white bread
- 150g thinly sliced beef (beef for gyu don)
- 1 small onion, sliced
- 1 tablespoon soy sauce
- 1 tablespoon mirin
- 1 teaspoon sugar
- Pickled ginger (optional)

Instructions:

1. In a pan, sauté the sliced onions until soft.
2. Add the thinly sliced beef and cook until browned.
3. In a bowl, combine soy sauce, mirin, and sugar to make a sauce, then pour it over the beef and onions.
4. Toast the bread lightly.
5. Place the beef and onion mixture on one slice of bread and top with pickled ginger (optional).
6. Close the sandwich and serve.